# WHEN the MOON RISES

Poems of the Womb

# CUANDO sale LA LUNA

Poemas de la Matriz

by

Leanna Day

Pacific Raven Press
Ka`a`awa, Hawai`i
www.pacificravenpress.co

© 2024 by Pacific Raven Press, LLC

All rights reserved. This book may not be reproduced, in whole or in part, including illustrations, in any form (beyond that copying permitted by Sections 107 and 108 of the U.S. Copyright Law and except by reviewers for the public press), without written permission from the publisher.

Pacific Raven Press, LLC
Ka`a`awa, Hawai`i 96730

**ISBN:** 978-1-7367287-1-0
**ISBN (ebook):** 978-1-7367287-3-4

Cover design and concept by Leanna Day and Nicholas Angiulo

Illustrations by Nicholas Angiulo and Judy Harbottle

Photograph on Back Cover by Cefestudio

Book layout by Jonathan Zane, Eien Design **www.eiendesignstudio.com**

Editor: Karla Brundage
Editorial Assistant: Mera Moore

This work is licensed under Pacific Raven Press, LLC.

Library of Congress Cataloging-in-Publication Data
*When the Moon Rises: Poems of the Womb (Cuando sale la Luna: Poemas de la Matriz)*
by Leanna Day
Catalogued as: Poetry, Social Science, Feminism, Self-Help

Printed in the United States of America

Pacific Raven Press, LLC, is an independent publisher.
**http://pacificravenpress.co/**
**pacificravenpress@yahoo.com**

# Table of Contents

Dedication .................................................................... vii
Acknowledgements ....................................................... ix
Foreword ...................................................................... xi
Preface ......................................................................... xv

## I. Hija de la Luna ................................................... 1
Revelation ..................................................................... 3
Genesis ......................................................................... 4
To Be a Woman ............................................................ 6
Big Mouth ..................................................................... 9
La Tierra es La Madre de Todas las Cosas ................. 10
Salt of the Moon ......................................................... 12
Fortress ....................................................................... 13
Con Mi Aliento Último ............................................... 15
The Romance of Friendship ....................................... 16
Switch Flip .................................................................. 17
Behind Closed Doors .................................................. 18
Follow Me Home ........................................................ 19
Bottle Park .................................................................. 21
Creature ...................................................................... 23
How Deep? .................................................................. 24
Stained ........................................................................ 25

Witness ..................................................................................27
Footsteps to Nowhere ..........................................................30
Savior ....................................................................................31
Red Sun Sinks into the Hills of Gold ................................32
Bleached Sky ........................................................................33
Ritual Shower ......................................................................34
What the Fuck .....................................................................35
It's Time ................................................................................37
Déjà Vu .................................................................................38
Elevated ................................................................................39
Curled in a Corner ..............................................................41
La Misma Mujer ..................................................................42
Same Woman .......................................................................43
A Call to Break Female Silence ..........................................44
Zipped Too Tight .................................................................46
No One Will Believe You ....................................................47

## II. Hermana de las Estrellas ........................................ 49
Moon Drive ..........................................................................51
Fairy Tales ............................................................................52
Ya Aquel Árbol no Florece Como Antes Florecía ...........53
Dakini ...................................................................................55
Levels of Poison ...................................................................56
Eaten By Worms ..................................................................57
Fertilizer ...............................................................................58
Ash Mirrors Rain .................................................................59
What If? ................................................................................61
Someone ...............................................................................62
Outgrown .............................................................................63
Sundown ..............................................................................65

To the Baby I'll Never Have.................................................66
To the Mother I'll Never Meet .............................................68
Loyal Bean ............................................................................69
Burnside................................................................................70
Disobedience.........................................................................72
Melting..................................................................................73
Rebirth ..................................................................................75
Prayer List.............................................................................76
Picture This...........................................................................77
Impotence.............................................................................79
Unspoken..............................................................................80
Blue Light..............................................................................81
Savasana................................................................................82
Breaking Away .....................................................................84
Finding Joy in the Day to Day ............................................85
Is Metaphor Enough?..........................................................86
Addictions ............................................................................87
Women of the Future ..........................................................88
After a Cookie......................................................................89
Out of Time..........................................................................91
Witches of the Bayou ..........................................................92

**III. Madre de los Planetas ............................................... 95**
Dinner at a Restaurant .......................................................97
Childhood Amnesia.............................................................98
Zeny's House ......................................................................101
Eating the Sun....................................................................103
Wax, Wane..........................................................................105
Nobody Wants a Cute Poem ............................................106
Mahina................................................................................107

| | |
|---|---|
| Not Knowing | 108 |
| Not a Martyr | 109 |
| La Víctima de Nadie: Una Fantasia? | 111 |
| Coming Home | 117 |
| Wasting Time | 119 |
| Grounding | 121 |
| Heart & Hunter | 122 |
| Maybe If My Mother | 123 |
| Crawling into a Vagina | 125 |
| Done | 126 |
| Everything's Bigger | 127 |
| We Are Witches | 128 |
| A Teacher for Life | 129 |
| Toes | 131 |
| Nothing | 132 |
| If I Could Find the Time | 134 |
| Hand to Mouth | 136 |
| I Think I Could Understand | 137 |
| A Piece of You | 139 |
| Because It Does | 140 |
| Golden-Brown Butter | 141 |
| Shuffling Cards | 142 |
| Cracking Open | 143 |
| The Baptism | 144 |
| When the Moon Rises | 145 |
| Note from the Author | 147 |

# Dedication

To those who have come before me
To those who are currently with me
To those who will follow after me

*A los que vineron antes de mí*
*A los que ahora están conmigo*
*A los que me seguirán*

# Acknowledgements

To each of my students, you shape me daily. You've been by my side through every step of this book's creation without knowing it. Thank you for clapping at the end of my classes, for constantly making me feel like I can move mountains, and for believing in me at a time when I thought I'd never believe in myself. I feel so lucky to have you.

To my husband, who has stood with me through every high and every low, there aren't enough words. Thank you for being my biggest cheerleader, pushing me to exist on my own agenda, and supporting my art when I couldn't myself.

To my best friends *old and new,* this book feels as much yours as it does mine. Thank you for holding me, for laughing with me, and for loving me through it all. You are mirrored in each of my poems, and I would not be me without you.

To my teacher, thank you for seeing and encouraging the things in me that I thought were extinct, for somehow accurately predicting my life over the last two years, and for telling me when to suck on a lemon.

To my parents, you will always be my muse. Mom,

thank you for teaching me to never settle and to remove my verbal filter when needed. Dad, thank you for teaching me to work hard and to be courageous in situations that make me uncomfortable.

To my publisher and editors at Pacific Raven Press, Kathryn, Karla, and Mera, it has been one of my life's great joys to work with you both. Thank you for believing in my vision, taking risks with me, and working tirelessly to refine this message. I thank my lucky stars that our paths ever crossed.

To the amazing artists who visually represent this book, *we did it!* I extend gratitude not only to my dear friend, Nicholas Angiulo, but also to my beloved mother, Judith Harbottle. Thank you both for seeing my words in a way that only you could.

To every woman who has ever been silenced or taken advantage of, I will fight for you with my last breath.

To the moon, thank you for being what I can always count on. I model my life after yours. The storms, the darkness, the comfort. I am forever yours.

I am eternally grateful. This book is not possible without you all.

# Foreword

## by Mary Angiulo
*(writer, artist, friend)*

You know that person in your life who you can get into the nitty gritty with, no matter the context? The one who shows up without judgment or the belief that they need to change you, but is simply there to listen? Leanna Day is that person for me, my penguin, my lobster, my water witcher. I've watched her journey from someone who shapes themselves for the world around them to the person making tsunamis, rather than waves, with the power she possesses. I feel very privileged to witness the person she has grown into, and continues to grow into.

The awakened woman, the ultimate mother, has been a large part of Leanna's healing journey. The Mother has set Leanna on a personal quest to grow and reflect in the act that comes most naturally to her, writing. Each of these poems is a collection of her journey from inner childhood healing to the trials and tribulations of adulthood as a woman in this world. Through her own healing journey, she aims to create space for those who remain confused and voiceless in spaces they feel they have no power in. She isn't afraid to go to the dark and scary places we hide deep inside. She has taken the ugly, guttural, throat tearing screams from deep inside and laid them out on a silver platter for our pleasure.

Leanna has studied many different cultural beliefs and practices, as well as sought out women from all different walks of life along her journey. *When the Moon Rises* is not only about her own healing, but also how women have influenced her along the way. This collection of poetry fights against the connections of chaos and oppression in a world too structured against feminine power. It creates a space where it is okay to say no, to smile at the man who calls you a bitch, to create healthy boundaries, and scream cathartic words. This isn't meant to be pretty; it is meant to be *real*. We are born of dirt, of ash and stardust, and we will return back to it. Leanna knows that though nature is beautiful, it doesn't care what you think. It is what it is meant to be, and through its beauty it can be a ravenous creature that will completely devour you. To understand what nature truly is, is to understand a lot more about what a person truly is. *When the Moon Rises* emphasizes getting back to nature, listening to yourself, finding that instinct, and opening your heart to it.

*When the Moon Rises* sits with you, the reader, wrapped in a hammock, crying over lemongrass tea while you tell the stories of your mother's mothers. This book is here to listen, to hear you yell, and encourage your voice. It will advocate for you, cherish your presence, and not ask you to make yourself smaller for anyone else. It is here for the good, the bad, and best of all, the ugly because it is real and raw. Don't hide from the truth of pain. Feel it and use it to grow in your own magic. These poems see you, hear your call, and come to you gladly because you are each other's sister, friend, mother, ally. *When the Moon Rises* will be with you through every cry, laugh, and scream, cherishing you as the gift that you are to this universe in every life you may live.

# Preface

*When the Moon Rises* is a very heavy book with explicit content. There are themes of violence, torture, gore, sexual assault, self-harm, and dangerous, depressive thoughts. Please take breaks when needed while reading this book, as much of its content can be triggering.

The darkest poems in this collection are *"No One Will Believe You"* and *"La Victíma de Nadie."* This book is heavily inspired by my mother, who was brave enough to not only share her story of sexual assault with me, but to also support my writing and inclusion of it for this collection. Knowing my audience will be able to relate, I take this very seriously. The poem *"La Victíma de Nadie"* was my way of having creative carte blanche, not holding anything back . . . to give her and other survivors some form of justice, of closure, and a sense that their stories matter.

Many of the poems involve bodily harm, graphic depictions, or violence. You, the reader, may be getting into something dark. If you do not feel ready, I encourage you to come back at a time when you do.

# WHEN *the* MOON RISES

Poems of the Womb

# CUANDO *sale* LA LUNA

Poemas de la Matriz

# I.
# HIJA de la LUNA
## *Daughters of the Moon*

# Revelation

I made this for you
    Because I know how mad you are
        I know why you hurt
            They did it to me too
                No one heard you back then ~ *I promise*
            But you're loud and clear now
        And I'm gonna fight for you
      Because you told me your story
                                And I won't let it go to waste

# Genesis

In the beginning, was the womb
    Within the womb, grew the world
        When the womb was ready, she birthed the world

    She said, "Let there be light," and the Moon flashed
        She said, "Let there be consciousness," and the tides grew
            "Let there be witches, goddesses, healers, and teachers"
                From her womb emerged
                      Witches, goddesses, healers, and teachers

Within the light
    Appeared alluring fruit
        It was called
            *Knowledge*

Fruit of power, of control, of assertion
        One season produced too much fruit
            And then another season
                And then another

        *Too much*
            *Of anything*
                *Is never*
                    *A good thing*

In the beginning, there was the womb

*These are the stories of her daughters*

# To Be a Woman

If you get raped, report it immediately
It's your fault if you don't say anything
But don't expect to be believed
You probably asked for it anyways

If you don't want kids
You're selfish
Get used to that weird look you'll get
Are you also a baby murderer?

If you want kids
Make sure your body bounces back immediately
If it doesn't, you're lazy
By the way, they'll only be happy for you if it's a boy

Wanna go back to work after kids?
That's selfish
Who's gonna be there for them?
'Cause no one's expecting dad to be

Don't wanna go back to work after kids?
Wow – Lazy
You probably just sit on the couch
Eating junk all day

Don't depend on a man
Make your own living

Crawl your way to the top
But they'll pay you less once you get there

If a man does provide for you
He'll remind you what he pays for
Making damn sure you
Don't forget

Shave every day because body hair is gross
But if the locks on your head aren't long and lush
You're not much of a woman
Now are you?

Also make sure your ass is round
Your tits are perky, tummy's tiny
And if you have acne
Just wash your face

Don't get angry
Never speak up
If you do, you're a crazy bitch
Also you should smile more

Wanna have safe sex? That probably makes you a whore
It's not his responsibility
So make sure to pump yourself full of hormones
Enjoy all the side effects for years to come

Don't expect him to ask you
What's on your mind
Can you just calm down, shut up
And watch tv?

Send nudes, but
Don't expect anything in return
And if he shows them to his friends
Take the blame for sending them in the first place

Get some filler
Go on a diet
Wear some lace
Keep things spicy

If you get abused
Why'd you stay?
Verbal sparring?
That's not real abuse

Why do you have postpartum depression?
You have this amazing baby!
Ungrateful and self-absorbed
Be sure to take care of it all night so he can sleep

If you're in pain
That he'll never know
Grow up
You're still expected to go to work and be sexy

Oh you're crying?
So dramatic
Stop being emotional
It's not cute

Did I miss anything?

# Big Mouth

They nicknamed me *Big Mouth*
*Ready, fire, aim- she doesn't think before she speaks*
They told me I needed to stop talking back

Do you think I ever listened?

For years, they tried to shut me up
*They're listening now*

# La Tierra es La Madre de Todas las Cosas

*The Earth Is the Mother of All Things*

The wind that blows
Through the leaves of the Tree
Is the silent witness
To the pain thrust upon Her

Stripped of Her fruit
Initials carelessly carved into Her flesh
She calluses the wounds
But will wear the scars forever

She provides breath, shelter, homestead
The powerhouse of our ecosystem
Turned into
Lumber, cigarette filters, dollar signs

Womb slashed with an axe
Left as nothing more than a stump
For money, power, and
15 seconds of demeaning, horrific, repulsive satisfaction

To fathom how strong
Her roots truly are
Is to realize
She is your Mother
And it's time to leave Her alone

# Salt of the Moon

and when the foam rolls in
to meet the sand against the shoreline
it's her
kissing my feet

# Fortress

My parents wanted to live in the middle of nowhere
A three-acre plot of land, where everyone got lost
Trying to find
My dad's friends called it his fortress

People said our house was scary – it was
Sounds of my parents' screams
Night terrors who still haunt
Watching me

As terrifying as it could be
I also found it magical
Where I could climb on top of the roof
Fall out of trees and bruise my butt
Soar on the tire swing
Burn my pinky on a gas lamp
Fish for tadpoles in the creek
Run through the woods as fast as I could
Lay on the earth without caring how dirty it made me

I still don't understand why
I was sad to move away
This weird connection between that place, me
*And wanting*
To escape
What happened inside those walls

Wanting to reframe bad memories into something positive
I now understand why
My parents wanted to live in the middle
Of nowhere
No buildings, highway noises, or overpopulation
Just Earth sounds and still, the freshest air
I've ever breathed

My first memory of nature's oasis
*Leanna's Fortress*

# Con Mi Aliento Último

## *With My Last Breath*

I'll love you like an artist
If it means I talk through my favorite songs

I'll love you like a Goddess
Showing you the feelings you didn't know you had

I'll love you like a witch
Running up a mountain
To hide during the new moon
Wanting you to follow

A new tattoo that reminds me of you
A sheet pan of roasted vegetables
Rosemary infused olive oil
A fight that lasts for hours
As long as we fall asleep in the same bed

Rest your head on my chest
I'm not going anywhere
Take your shoes off
Walk in the grass with me, where

*I'll love you like a woman*

# The Romance of Friendship

I was exhausted
And you felt comfortable

You saw the scabs
I had yet to find on myself
But you never picked at them
Because walls don't come down that way

When you bleed, I bleed
The presence of a person
Who makes you want to listen to your belly
When it grumbles for food…*the first time*

You talk until your face is blue
But I cling to every word because
When your throat starts to vibrate
*I can feel the earth shake*

When you chase the rain, I'll follow
When you flop on the couch to groan, I'll be there too

Meeting you again

Mother
Anchor
Sister
Home

# Switch Flip

Overwhelmed
Not knowing what to think
Still trying to express

My eyes begin to flood
I try to stop it
But that only makes it worse

I saw a switch flip on your face
*The moment you stopped taking me seriously*

Did you ever
*Really*
Take me seriously *in the first place?*

# Behind Closed Doors

Grown men
Touch
Little girls

# Follow Me Home

I'd be the chasm you stepped over
when an earthquake split the ground

The choiceless pit of dread
sprouting dandelions on a good day

The line stuck in your head
from the song you can't remember

*Imagine being held by me*

                        as I fall from the sky
                hoping the clouds will catch me
              don't cry for me – it's too tiring
       the second attempt and then the fourth
      by the twelfth, we've all stopped caring

I'd be the myth of moving on
when you can't bear to let go

The last breath of fresh air
in the depths of your backyard landfill

The sweet feeling of escape
when you pry your feet from the mud

*I am imagining you*

                      while I fall from the sky
                begging the clouds to catch me
don't cry for me – I can do that on my own
        the second attempt and then the fourth
    by the twelfth, we've all stopped breathing

# Bottle Park

*Dedicated to my late grandfather,
Rick Harbottle*

We used to boop our noses together
Yours was the perfect button
Warm, round, and red like a cherry

Today, you are laid out on a table
A man uncovers the blanket to reveal
Your perfect face and purple nose
Cold when I touch it

I never thought *I'd* have to be the strong one
For my big sister
Having never seen her cry like this
I stand there – blank, frozen, shocked
But I stand
Because the three of us, together
Would've made you happy
Happier than driving a houseboat

In a few years,
I'll marry the guy who dad hates right now
*They wind up really liking each other*
On my wedding day

I'll wear the little sapphire ring
You bought for Mamaw on your honeymoon

I recount to my niece and nephew
Stories of the one-eyed, one-horned, flyin' purple
People eater
I take up plants and collecting Santa trinkets
My grandma says I'm turning into her
It's nice to think that I have something in common
To the woman you loved

You're here
Though I can't dye your mustache purple anymore
Or kick your floaty seat from underneath you at the lake
You're living within me
I'll cherish those last couple voicemails
Forever

# Creature

I look at my hands
I wonder whose they really are

Will the nightmares ever stop?

I feel like the creature from *The Ring*
Crawling out of that forgotten well

Every time I think I'm close to the top
I slip and fall back to the cold floor

I look at my fingernails
Splitting and tearing away from my skin

And I wonder whose they really are
Because they certainly don't feel like mine

What truly feels like mine
Is the pain from the rip
The never-ending climb
Towards someone else's bright life

# How Deep?

Why do we tell children to *control* their emotions
When what we really mean is

*Suppress them*

# Stained

I was cleaning spilled wax

The purple dye from the candle
Stained my nightstand

I looked at the spot nearby
Where I once lit an incense cone
But didn't place anything underneath
To protect the surface

I thought about how my dad
Likes his house to look
As if no one lives there

Is the purple stain a blemish?
Is the burn mark a flaw?

Or is it a story?

A story of how I lived
Without striving for perfection

A story of how I wasn't afraid
To negate a rigid set of rules

A story of how I learned
To refute the belief
That I ruin everything I touch

The stain and the burn
Mementos of my journey
A path to self-acceptance

# Witness

A crashing sound came from the garage, followed by her screams. With a war continuing in his head, laughter was few and far between these days.

A small girl ran to investigate, freezing once she reached the doorway. She was followed by her smaller sister, who stood on tiptoe for a better look. **There it was.**

She, cornered, pinned, lion's prey. Using her long fingernails like the teeth of a fork, raked into his jaw, making sure he knew this was not a game she would play idly, no matter the shade of blue her skin might turn.

*But what if he was trying to calm her down? A singular scene is not a full story. Seemingly cut and dry, lines become blurred when taking into account the years that led up to this moment. What if he never started it? What if he did? What if they took each other, for better or for worse, until the day they just couldn't?*

She yelled to the girls with the force of a hundred ancestors behind her throat, "Call the police! Call the police!" – trying to pull away from the riptide of his arms. He, an immovable stone, holding her shoulders, silent. Frozen in the gravity of the small eyes upon him.

"Do it," little sister whispered, with as much vigor as she could muster. "Do it," a little louder this time.

A dormant cocoon, not a butterfly, big sister was preserved in a cloud of shock. Paralyzed by visions of court rooms, painful orphanages, unwanted goodbyes, and the knowing that *those two* loved each other almost as much as they loved their girls.

Haze of the moment, the four were suddenly huddled in a bathroom. They assured the girls everything was okay. Little sister looked away, catching a glimpse of *Maya and Miguel* playing on the Spongebob TV in her nearby bedroom. The mother in the show said something about the North Star always being a guide back home. She was as sure of this cosmic ability as the four of them were that . . . this wasn't the end.

That night, big sister held her smaller half, her first baby. Little sister awoke to music coming from the living room. She tiptoed away from big sister's bed, following the sound of "Last Call" by Lee Ann Womack singing from the speakers of her SpongeBob CD player. That same mix of sad, country love songs she wished she wasn't so familiar with.

A peek through the doorway, **and there they were.** On the blue fabric couch, beneath a blanket that wasn't quite big enough for the two of them, she lay asleep in his arms, his chin resting on her hairline. *Between an overwhelmed man and a misunderstood woman, both hurting, the only villain here is the danger of a single-sided story.*

They had forgiven each other . . . for now.

# Footsteps to Nowhere

The ballad of my life
Was that I saw violence
In both of them
It took years to admit
It continued through me
So the chorus became
Running away
To the oasis I built
Where it's safe
A thousand miles from anyone

                                                                 Footsteps

*And then you knocked*

# Savior

I remember touching myself when I was young
Then praying for forgiveness afterward

Because pleasure is saved for marriage
Everybody knows that
You're supposed to give that part of yourself
To your husband and no one else
*Not even you*

Just how the fuck is a kid
Supposed to learn about themselves?
What they like, what they don't
*While Jesus watches and Satan smiles*

I can't think of a safer way
A less judgmental way
A more self-loving way
To explore your own body

Instead, I was taught
By the racist, sexist, Southern Baptists
To recite the books of the Bible
To the tune of "Ten Little Indians"

Yeah, I found Jesus
*The Devil is a master of disguise*

# Red Sun Sinks into the Hills of Gold

They found each other as a safe haven
When the pale gray moon shined on a dead man
Untainted by the inhumanities of the world
When the cold black sky shadowed a dead woman
Innocent to the force of man's wandering hand

They built a home of straw
Used everything they owned
But wolves destroy weak houses
And they both died alone

Your cup runneth over?
Mine isn't filled to the brim
He's got blood on his hands
So tell your God I'm mad at him

# Bleached Sky

Watching dust from a bleached sky
I remembered the way my stomach felt
At the thought of going back

Like that ride at the fair
Where you rise along a vertical tower
And you hang out at the top
Just long enough for your heart to smack your sternum
Like a hand against a drum

Only there was no funnel cake in my future

No squiggly lines or crispy exterior
No dusting with so much powdered sugar
It disguises the mess beneath

Fairs are fun, but
At some point
I had to go back
Where I wouldn't count on anyone to win me a teddy bear
Because I wanted to win it *myself*

# Ritual Shower

In your bathroom
Turn off the lights
*Use candles instead*
Burn an incense stick
Play your music loud enough to hear from the shower
Something slow and sexy
*My favorite*
Make your water hot and cozy
*Step in*
Let your neck sway from side to side
Roll your shoulders
Swing your hips back and forth
Massage your temples
Exfoliate your skin from head to toe
*And take your time*
Step out
Anoint yourself with oil
Mix in your favorite scents
Blow a kiss in the mirror to the Goddess you see
*There – now you're glowing*

# What the Fuck

Being told, *You look like your Dad*
I was always offended to favor that bald guy
With wide pores, thick cheeks, and two deep lines between his brows

I heard boys talk about his terrifying eyes
But he never scared me
Then again, I think he knew he never could

Eventually I started hearing about my resting bitch eyes
How I always looked ready to fight
*Unapproachable,* they said
A *what the fuck* face

I noticed wrinkles in the mirror
Deep and gaping – I'd seen these before
*I'm too young for this,* I thought
Too young for two cavernous lines between my brows
Ugly, masculine, needing filler
Wrinkles more pronounced than my mother's
Who is 31 years my senior
*Why can't I have her skin?*

One night, walking alone through a sketchy part of town
I wondered how many situations
My *what the fuck* wrinkles have saved me from

Then I canceled the Botox appointment

# It's Time

They question why women stay silent
But they never ask who put the duct tape over our mouths in the first place

They tag us as erratic
During a pissing match over who touches the moon first

They want us to remember how they provide
When they've forgotten *their* breath comes from *our* womb

They tell the apocalypse cameras they're on our side
While behind the lens, they make sure we suffocate under the rubble

They've groomed us to believe we're imperfect
And I need to make sure you know

**YOU ARE THE CANVAS**
**YOU ARE THE MEDIUM**
**YOU ARE THE PAINTER**
**YOU ARE THE ART HERSELF**

*And it's time to be angry*

# Déjà Vu

Sometimes I'll get my skin too close to a flame and think
*Strange, familiar*
*I've burned like this before*

Other times, I'll stand up to flush the toilet
Notice the deep shade of cranberry the water's turned
And think

*Oh no, I forgot to package it up to send to the world leaders*

# Elevated

My mom loves flavored water

She infuses her glass
With anything she can find

*Mint*
*Strawberries*
*Lemon*
*Rosemary*

No two glasses
Are ever the same

When she finishes her drink
She gets a little snack

I used to think it was weird
Unnecessary
Soggy

Until I realized it's art

The creative elixir
She nourishes herself with

Is an act of self-praise
Because *why* shouldn't she
Be treating herself
To fancy water
Every day?

# Curled in a Corner

old dog didn't do much
but curl into hidden corners
better to be invisible
than to keep getting hurt

thirteen years in and out of a concrete slab
old dog had rotting teeth and achy bones
they thought he would wither away in there
and so did he

one day, some people gave him a bed
and another bed, and another
then they took old dog to a new place
with a roof and more food and soft beds in every corner

they cleaned his teeth and soothed his bones
and pretended not to see when he stole treats
then they promised old dog
he'd never sleep on concrete again

# La Misma Mujer

## *Versión en Español*

Soy el cristal de la tierra
Tu eres la hija de la luna

Agarro el huevo cósmico de la creación en mi mano
Tu agarras las estrellas para pintar las constelaciones

Somos la magia nacida de nuestra madre
De nuestra abuela
De cada útero de nuestro linaje

No venimos de ninguna costilla del hombre
*No me hagas reír*

Estamos aquí
Estamos en todas partes
No nos vamos a mover

Somos las mujeres que éramos hace milenios atrás
*Pero aprendimos algunas cosas nuevas*

# Same Woman

## *English Version*

I am the crystal of the earth
You are the daughter of the moon

I hold the cosmic egg of creation in my hand
You hold the stars to paint constellations

We are the magic birthed by our mother
Our grandmother
Every womb in our lineage

We came from no man's rib
*Don't make me laugh*

We are here
We are everywhere
We will not move

We are the same women we were millennia ago
*But we've learned some new things*

# A Call to Break Female Silence

I had just put my class into a 12-minute *savasana*
Yoga pose
Like a bad teacher, I checked my email
*Acceptance for Publication*
I'm confused
*Your manuscript has been reviewed and recommended for publication by two of our editors*
I forgot how to blink
*As a woman-owned small press, we are quite moved by the themes you present about shifting the*
*paradigm of patriarchy and abuse to empowerment, a call to break female silence*
That has a nice ring to it

Knowing exactly how to celebrate
Because I was ovulating and it was spring and the moon was dark and
*Everything was about to change*
After class, in the car, I screamed every song
Then I went to the beach
I just knew
All the little sand crabs were dancing behind me
When I told the moon

Believe it if you want to
Or write it off as poetic metaphor
Three *massive* waves crashed into my hips
The Hindu female trinity *Tridevi*
Was hugging me

As my feet sank deeper into the sand
I sang that stupid Kenny Chesney song
*Now I know how Jimmy Buffet feels*
Then I drove home too fast
Because I couldn't wait to tell my dogs
I not-so-shamelessly sang
*Now I know how Richard Petty feels*

A call to break female silence
I *really* like the sound of that

*Now I know how Maya Angelou feels*
*Now I know how Rupi Kaur feels*
*Now I know how Adrienne Rich feels*
*Now I know how Julia Alvarez Feels*

# Zipped Too Tight

The nylon trimming
Sewn into skin
Showcases the shiny metal teeth
Climbing up the center of a girl
Whose body keeps a secret
Her brain has yet to find

A tiny bone handle
Dangles between her lips
Unzip, only if
You can stomach
The stories you'll find

# No One Will Believe You

I'd never been to a gynecologist before
They called me back
My mom stood up
They waved a hand at her to stay seated
I was to go inside the exam room alone.

After the door closed, a doctor gave me an order
                       *Quítate la ropa* (Take off your clothes)
I didn't know doctors were supposed to
Give you a gown and leave the room
He didn't hand me a gown
He didn't leave the room
He stood there *watching*
I started to tremble
                                      *Relájate* (Relax)
But I couldn't
                               *Acuéstate* (Lie down)
I started to cry
                *Necesitas relajarte* (You need to relax)
But I couldn't
      *Voy a hacer que te relajes* (I'm going to make you relax)
I closed my eyes
When I opened them . . .

Do you want me to say it?

Others are too chickenshit, don't want to hear
They say be nice, pretend it never happened
I wish I could do that

On that exam table
With my legs up in stirrups
HE RAPED ME RAW – SAY IT OUT LOUD
I tried to fight, tried to run
But he pushed me harder into the table and whispered
                *Nadie te creer*á (No one will believe you)
To be a blinded deer frozen in time
Can't see his face, only his bald head
Afterward, he tossed me a towel and a tube of ointment
Towel for the blood, ointment for the rash
The rash I was there for in the first place

My mom asked how it went
I showed her the ointment
*This is the story of how I ended up in an abortion clinic*

# II.
# Hermana de las Estrellas

*Sister of the Stars*

# Moon Drive

When the voice in your head
Leaves such deep scars
That you misplace your ability to make a simple decision

Who's left to blame?

If I drive until I forget the moon is blue
Maybe I'll remember what it's like to trust myself
What if I tell it to the stars?
Will they believe me?
When the rain finally washes me away
Maybe then

I'll sleep through the night

# Fairy Tales

What if grandma's house
Was a symbol of adulthood?

What if the wolf
Was a symbol of the man you never want to meet?

What if the red hood
Was a symbol of innocence?

What if he sighed on your neck
Covered your mouth with his hand
Made you touch it until it was hard
Put his mouth between your legs
And called it a game?

# Ya Aquel Árbol no Florece Como Antes Florecía

*The Tree Doesn't Flower Like It Used To*

I thought depression would leave once I got over the freak who touched me when I was little, but depression doesn't work that way. Instead, it looks like having the most amazing afternoon yet, full of laughter and beauty and "How is the world so astounding?"

Then waking up the next day, struggling to feed yourself, feeling like an incompetent waste of space who will never amount to anything, knowing that thinking that way and talking to yourself that way only makes everything worse, but it's hard – it's so fucking hard not to and it's even harder to pull yourself out of that hole so you smoke it away to distract yourself and it works for a while before you realize you can't do that forever – you're just cheating yourself.

Depression didn't come and go with the freak whose face I still cannot see. It's always been here. The guest who holds the record for "most overstayed welcome" in history.

So you're back scrolling mindlessly on your phone, unable to stand in front of the mirror because you don't recognize the face staring back at you and you feel guilty – you feel so fucking guilty because there are people out there who are starving, who don't have nearly as much as you do. For Christ's sake, have you ever read *I Know Why the Caged Bird Sings?*

And you know you're lucky and you feel like a piece of shit for not being more grateful. Therefore, you do not deserve to feel worthless.

Feeling – feeling anything is amazing – it's a miracle because it means you're alive and it makes you appreciate the high highs that much more, but why – *why* do the low lows have to hurt so much?

So you hide under a blanket because at least here, no one can see how brittle you are. But eventually, that pounding voice in your head comes screaming, "What the hell are you gonna do with your life? You can't live this way forever."

Can you?

# Dakini

No man can contain you
Like an octopus
You thrive off raw instinct
Try as they may
*No one can quite figure you out*

# Levels of Poison

Am I actually drowning
Or am I making it up?

Why can't I just be content?
Why must I be addicted to feeling like shit?

Is it a cry for attention?
Don't I already get enough of that?

Am I poison to my home
Just here to ruin things?

What do I actually have to be upset about?
Why am I even here?

I'm tired
I'm so tired

What must've happened
To make me feel this worthless?
Every
Fucking
Second

# Eaten By Worms

Spit on my face and hurt me

No, I won't say a word

It's not you, it's me

I shouldn't have

You deserve to be angry

I don't – I get it

I forced you to be this way

I'm making up stories to get your attention

I'm sorry

Carry me out back

And tuck me under the dirt

I'm cozy here

The worms are my friends

No one else can have me

*I'm yours*

# Fertilizer

When leaves begin to yellow
They have to be pruned
To make room for new growth

*A part of me had to die*
*In order for other parts to bloom*

# Ash Mirrors Rain

Through ink and the moon
Ash and rain
Bloody toilet bowls
Water merging into sand

I found you

The one who held me last summer
When I remembered the things I was afraid to say out loud

The one who told me to forget about sleep hygiene
Take a goddamn nap – if it's the only real sleep I get this week

The one who took me to the beach every day I was overstimulated
Stuck me in the water
Told me to dance because *who gives a shit* if anyone sees

The one who fed me boxes upon boxes
Of Domino's marbled cookie brownies
When you could see more of my ribs than you could my belly
Asking, *why don't they just call it a brookie?*

For you
I'll do better tomorrow

I'm trying to be better
For you

It's hard
I'm tired
Sometimes I feel so stuck
I don't even know who I am

But for you, I promise
I'll stand in front of the *mirror*
And until I believe it, I'll say

Through ink and the moon
Ash and rain
Bloody toilet bowls
And the way water merges into sand

I'm finding *me.*

# What If?

I tell my sister about all the hours I'm putting in
The shadow work, rituals, meditation, hypnosis
To remember the man who touched me
What he looked like
Where he did it
How old I was
Why it happened at all

*What if you don't remember?*
She asks

*What if you never remember*
*And you hurt yourself in the process?*

                                                               Too late

# Someone

*You need to eat, baby*
*I can see your ribs*

He stares at me sitting in water
The bath he drew
For me
The flicker of the candle he lit
Dances over my deflated breasts
I'm so tired

*I think you're depressed,* he says

I'm not offended
Numb, maybe, but – relieved, mostly

                        Because at least someone believes me now

# Outgrown

here for now, gone tomorrow
to the wet, sticky, Seminole air
where i'll run away from mom

here for now, gone tomorrow
to Humphreys Peak
where i'll run away from dad

here for now, gone tomorrow
to the dry, dusty desert
where i'll hide from a dream

here for now, gone tomorrow
back to a painful place
where i'll run to a boy

*something else*
*always on the horizon*
*the escapist*

here for now, gone tomorrow
to a fixer upper in the sticks
where i'll watch my parents crumble apart

here for now, gone tomorrow
sitting in a church pew
where i'll watch the Devil lurk behind a pulpit

here for now, gone tomorrow
off to . . . somewhere
where . . . something . . . m*ight* happen

here for now, gone tomorrow
another new classroom
where from a corner, i'll watch them be alive without me

> *she who sees*
> *the fly on the wall*
> *here, and there . . . and where?*

here for now, gone tomorrow
away forever
where some places hurt too much to return

here for now, gone tomorrow
to cowboy country
where brisket should only ever be

here for now, gone tomorrow
biting into a juicy peach
where i'll meet mindfulness and kiss her goodnight

here for now, gone tomorrow
swimming through the pacific
where i'll start finding a home . . . within myself

> *just that – a place*
> *and sometimes*
> *that's all it needs to be*

# Sundown

Last night I dreamt I lit a candle on the roof
And I didn't need to explain myself anymore

Walking through "Nights in White Satin"
Detachment taught by wind

To live in ritual meant
Finding beauty in a sea of mundanity

Last night I dreamt I lit a candle on the roof
This time, I allowed myself to believe
Everything would be okay

*I* was going to make it that way

# To the Baby I'll Never Have

If I'm being completely honest
I don't want you
It's still weird to face the reality
That now, I'll never have you

The world is a scary place
I want to protect you from it
I don't want it to hurt you
*I* don't want to hurt you

I refuse to follow my parent's footsteps
Thinking a child would heal me
*That isn't fair*

I've got too much work to do in this life, baby
I can't carry all of it
*And you*
At the same time

I choose to heal myself first
I like to believe
The world will heal a little
As a result

I'm trying to make this place a better home for you
I hope you understand

Maybe I'll hold you in my next life
For now, my baby
I love you
So I have to let you go

# To the Mother I'll Never Meet

I won't grow in your belly
Never suck on your breast
You'll never hold my hand
Or hug me when I cry

To tell you the truth,
In this lifetime at least
You are not a mother
I am not yours

*And that's okay*

I want to thank you
For being aware enough to *not* bring me into your life
Just because people said you were supposed to have me

Maybe another time
We'll be ready for each other

For now
If you love me
Let me go

# Loyal Bean

Feets that smell like corn chips
Scratchy tongue against my cheek
Nubby tail wagging 1,000 mph
Barks and squeaks translate to
*I'm so happy you're home! I missed you so much!*
Floppy ears
I swear she's smiling
Furry belly
Familiar
My best friend

The goodest girl

# Burnside

*Dedicated to my late grandfather,*
*Rick Harbottle*

when forgetting a life jacket taught me how to swim
*The Dale Hollow Lake held me*

when I hid from the one-eyed, one-horned, flyin, purple
people eater
*Dale Hollow held me*

when seeing the neighbor's pink Cadillac meant *we were
here* and I'd finally be able to sleep
*Dale Hollow held me*

when he gave me his soap to bathe in the lake
when I was queen of the world, sitting in his captain's chair,
steering that massive wheel
when he invested 100% of himself in the act
of making me laugh

when I got too afraid to call because it meant
facing what was next
*Dale hollow held me*

when his burned body sunk to the bottom of the lake
*Dale Hollow held me*

when the wound didn't leave but just became bearable
*Dale Hollow held me*

and when the whiff of a marina takes me back
to his boat slip

*Dale Hollow, **hold me***

# Disobedience

I was the first to sin
The first to eat the fruit
The first who refused
To blindly follow a man's orders

After I bit
What I saw, was truth – corrupted by a shadow
in the clouds
The snake became my friend
She followed me around like a pet

That god didn't create the universe
*I did*
That god wasn't tortured
*I was*
That god wasn't resurrected
*I came back from the dead*

I was the first to sin
And I'd do it again

# Melting

I remember her in the kitchen. Never being able to make just enough for two small mixed girls who ate like canaries, but rather, cooking for an army of *gringos* who had yet to experience Goya seasoning and *achiote* paste.

I remember being the only one of my friends who knew what a *guayaba* was, and certainly the only one who ate halved *maracuyá* for breakfast.

I remember the rush of excitement swelling in my belly when I walked inside to the smell of twelve-hour simmered *lentejas* or *arvejas*. Never, still, being able to decide which be my favorite.

I remember silently admiring but loudly laughing at her thick accent, her refusal to say "beach" or "sheet" as her *E* sounds so often came across as *I* sounds.

I remember her use of soy sauce. Not traditionally Panamanian, but something she picked up from her love of Chinese food, no matter how much it tore her stomach apart.

I remember hearing talk of *tostones* outside my home, but I only knew them as *patacones*.

I remember guarding the refrigerated *bolitas de tamarindo*

with my life, though I seemed to be the only one who really wanted them. Blessed with the foreign *dulce* just once or twice a year, I would savor the thick, gritty goop as slowly as I could, sourness scrunching my lips together, before spitting out the woody seed.

I remember the men who told her to go back to where she came from if she couldn't speak their language. How she knew more words in their tongue than they'd ever know in hers. Their blindness, never realizing that "home of the brave" sounds quite fit for someone who left their mother country.

# Rebirth

That rage is sacred
Should you be so lucky to feel it
It was never meant to be erratic or abusive
The way they conditioned you to believe
Anger means *you have something to say*
Not everyone gets that luxury
So use it
*Like a womban*
Because change never happened through silence

# Prayer List

do not put my name
on your prayer list
I don't need Jesus
*he needs me*

# Picture This

**Picture this**

You're 15 years old
Your biggest regret in life is being born with a vagina
You were caught listening to a song that chanted
*Woman/Life/Freedom*

**Picture this**

Now you're in a cell
Crying through a ceremony
Betrothing you to the 40-year-old man
Who is about to murder you

**Picture this**

But before he can pull out his gun
*He must RAPE you*
Because you're a virgin
Otherwise, he'll go to hell for killing you
Now that you're his wife
You're fair game

**Picture this**

They take your sister's freedom
They take your mother's life
They take your daughter's womb

**Picture this**
You chop off your hair
Torch your scarf
Spit in *his* face, telling *him* what to do

                                      What helps more
                                   Support or revenge?

# Impotence

Divine feminine
You think you want her
Because she's sexy on Instagram
The truth is
You can't handle her

You want someone with a pretty face
Who won't ask the hard questions
Or call you out on your bullshit

Basically
You want a sex trophy
What can you contribute?
When everything you learned about sex
Came from a screen
Behind a locked door
With you on your back
Expecting nothing more
Than to be served your ugliest desires

*Sounds hot*

Your obtuse construct of a divine feminine
Is the reason why you'll spend your life
Thinking of her in bed
*Never being lucky enough to feel her warmth*

# Unspoken

Tired of looking at bodies
Determining worth
By a fat ass
Clear skin
And a nicely held handstand

Backhanded, belittling comments
Trying to look
Like *his* advertisement

        Body hair
           Cellulite
              Acne
                  Stretch marks

                    Motifs of an experienced woman, *not a child*

You didn't get to choose

Your body
Is just a vehicle
Rented from the universe in this lifetime

Your body is the most boring thing about you
Meanwhile you've hidden the map of your soul

*Can you hear me?*

# Blue Light

Question why
We go outside
To be encompassed by nature

Instead of looking up
We hunch our necks down

*Enchanted*
By that electronic fucking rectangle in our hands

# Savasana

Go outside today

Look at that tree
Can you believe how massive it is?
How its branches and leaves
Design the perfect canopy
For you to sit beneath
How its thick bark
Constructs the perfect back rest to support you

Doesn't it make you feel small?

Go outside today

Listen to the generations of birds
The stories they have to tell
Tales of adventure
Soaring through winds
Exploring the world unseen

Doesn't it make you feel small?

Go outside today

Who cares about the fly
That landed on your arm?
Did it really hurt anything?

Let the wind mess up your hair

The earth never tried to be perfect
And look how unbelievable she is

The Earth never tried to be perfect
So why should you?

# Breaking Away

An authentic woman
Tape slapped on her mouth
Shoved in a closet
Lock on the door
Left to rot

*Angry*

At a society built around oppression
Having been groomed to believe
That rage means *she* needs to calm down

*Angry*

Because her mother never got to be

Once shoved in a closet
Now howling under the moon
*Angry*

She does not fight masculinity with masculinity
Rather, speaks body-shaking words
Enunciating screams sewn deep into skin

What can you stomach today?
Because she is sick of this shit

# Finding Joy in the Day to Day

Few things
Make me quite as happy
As a good poop story

# Is Metaphor Enough?

You glue your lips to mine

I sew my hand to yours

Are they

Ripping apart?

# Addictions

When I stepped in the water, the Eagle River asked
*Whose fault is it today?*

I shot a 20-year-old memory into my veins
When the wind whispered
*You've recycled that story twice this week already*

I found a flat, smooth rock
Watched it skip until the final splash muttered
*You pushed every last one of them away*

My rippling reflection knew what I'd never admit
*At some point, you have to accept responsibility*

                              so what do you do
                     when there's no one left to blame
                 do you roll your eyes at the habit
                       point the finger *again*
                                    or
                       do you roll up your sleeves
                           put in the work
                   to make it to the other side
                knowing it is never too late

# Women of the Future

I am a woman of the future
Soaring through space and time
I run with the stars
Bounce among the planets
I'm not sure what I'm searching for
But I know that it's mine
Maybe I lost it a while ago
Now, I follow the twists and pulls in my stomach
Trusting that I intuitively know where it is
My thinking mind is only in my way

I am a woman of the cosmos
Hitching a ride on the comet
Who offers herself to me
We're flying so quickly
I wonder if we'll crash into an asteroid
*It's not up to me*
We come upon a constellation
She drops me off, then glides on her way
The stars morph into breasted creatures
Who form a circle around me as I hear

*We've been waiting for you*

# After a Cookie

It was the year I learned that money would never make me feel successful

It was the year I learned that I *always* think better after a cookie

That I make excuses to rest . . . but I don't actually need an excuse

I learned to listen to my gut when it pulls me in directions I don't understand

Accept the parts of myself I stuffed away for so long

Trash everything that doesn't authentically inspire me and say yes **only** if it's a *holy hell yes*

It was the year I overwhelmed myself with houseplants . . . but I grew a guava tree

I confirmed I definitely do not want children . . . but that's not to say I haven't become a mother in my own way

It was the year I bought a needle with some ink and poked permanent leaves into my foot

Started looking in the mirror and seeing a little girl who was hurting and confused and *it was the year I took the time to hold her instead of ignore her*

It was the year I realized that the problem wasn't me, but rather, my environment, and –
whenever I went where I *wanted* to be – people followed

I discovered that being angry is one of my greatest gifts

I got so damn tired of holding on to things that only pulled me backward and through gritted teeth, I learned to let go

It was the year I decided to treat every period like it's Christmas Fuckin Eve

It was the year I started to figure out how to be proud of the skin I live in . . . *just as I am*, and I *don't* need to change anything

It was maybe my best year of all. But I've got a feeling I'm walking into something better.

# Out of Time

When the fuck
Did I decide
I *wasn't* powerful?

# Witches of the Bayou

Today, I'm having fun
Tonight, I'm going hunting

I swing in my hammock
Gazing at the tree above
Savoring every succulent bite
Of this season's sweet nectarine

I take a trip to the ocean
Throw a ball across the sand
Watching Nala splash in the water
As Smitty sprawls out
Not caring if the sun burns his little snout

I close my eyes and dance
To my newest bluegrass obsession
No, not *the man of constant sorrow*
Rather, *the witches of the bayou*

I pick herbs from my garden
For special batch of tea
Lemongrass, rosemary, sage, and mint
I smile because I can't wait to give my friend a taste

I smoke a little weed
To reward myself for writing
*Inhaling . . . exhaling*

Don't ask questions
Stay out of my way

Today, I feel alive
Because tonight, I'm going hunting
*For a man who hurt a girl*

# III.
# Madre de los Planetas

*Mother of the Planets*

# Dinner at a Restaurant

The charcoal circles beneath her eyes
Make her look *much older* than she is
Trapped in an adolescent's body
Notches between her legs
Tell a *much older* story
A sneaky hand slithers around her waist
Making her shoulders clench
    *Not here, not now*
She slides a couple inches away
Desperately hoping to avoid his touch

Fingers, not so much
More like – five snakes attached to a palm
Go hunting through her scalp
For the youthful nectar
That was stolen from her long ago
*Mom's in the dark, brother's always clueless*
Before thinking, her head jerks away
Accompanied by the swat of her wrist, but
She's a meal on a plate
Being pulled towards the hands she cannot control

*No one knows it*
*Yet somebody saw*

# Childhood Amnesia

Let's say he called it a game, and it tickled at first

I don't know how old I was
I can't see his face
I can tell you where he put his mouth
*But I don't really think I need to*

At 25, I laughed
With my partner's face between my thighs
After one swift lick to the right
I was in tears telling him to *back off*

Suddenly, I was a little girl again . . . a *little girl*
That face between my legs
Wasn't the person I married
Rather, a nauseating adult *who was supposed to know better*

I couldn't even speak, much less make sense of it
My cramped chest and gaping eyes kept repeating
*What the fuck just happened?*
*Why did it feel so familiar?*

My husband did everything he was supposed to
Apologized, apologized, apologized
Asked permission before touching me again
Covered me with a blanket and held me while I cried

You know what's hard as fuck to say out loud?
*I think a grown man touched me when I was a little girl*
*I'm ashamed to say it*
*Because I don't completely remember*

I fought about telling people
I fought about writing this down
I fought about looking myself in the mirror to admit it
*Until I thought about a girl*

The one who has her suspicions too
The one who doubts her body
The one who thinks she's fucking crazy *like I did*
I need her to know she's not alone

*This is not where our story ends*

I picture her face . . . and I see a little girl
Whose hands I desperately want to hold while whispering
*I'm fighting for you*
*I'm fighting for us*

People will step on the earth and know *it is our body*
    Swim in the ocean and know *it is our blood*
    Warm their skin against a fire and know *it is our power*

> Feel the wind through their hair and know *it is our breath*
> Gaze at a star and know *it is our voice*

Today, we are unbound, unchained, unstoppable, a*nd they know it*

# Zeny's House

*Ah! then, how dear the Muse's favours cost,*
*If those paint sorrow best--who feel it most!*
**Charlotte Smith, "Sonnet I"**

Bones rot
Lungs turn black
Fuzz grows on intestines

If I didn't ache
If you didn't gag at the necrotic stench
Of my decomposing body

Would you know I'm here?

My strengths mutilate me

My poison
My own spit

Gifted with pain
Gifted with a loud mouth
Gifted so you would *shut up* and *listen*

Slit my throat

The blood that spews
From the gash
Leaks the words that we wish weren't true

Vomit into my own hands

The leftover chunks that don't slip
Between my fingers
Show the fight for something better

# Eating the Sun

> *don't undress my love*
> *you might find a mannequin:*
> *don't undress the mannequin*
> *you might find*
> *my love.*
> Charles Bukowski, "Trapped"

Bukowski said it best
*Love Is a Dog from Hell*

I'm doing it again
making up flaws
holding dead hands
ashamed
I don't deserve love

Looking in the gutters
for suicides
Neglecting lavender scented bridges
I'm more than able to cross

Flesh covers bone
Nails claw
tear
dig

scratch
until nothing is left
nothing but dust

Easy to die
Easier, still, to fall apart

The phone rings
while I search for words
to ease my blustering mind
truthfully, I somehow crave
those demented, seething flaws
I crush up and form in a line to snort

To keep my love at bay
To keep my love away

Bukowski said it best

# Wax, Wane

When the sameness starts to itch
There's nothing left to pick apart

*It's time to stay when you want to leave*

When it's easier to be bold and alone like the moon
But you know the tides have to touch someone's feet

*It's time to stay when you want to leave*

When crying over the toilet means you're alive
Everything you ran from comes back
Chunkier and slimier than your last meal did

*It's time to stay when you want to leave*

When you look at the starry sky and don't see her
You know she's still there

*It's time to stay when you want to leave*

# Nobody Wants a Cute Poem

This version of you is my favorite

The one confused
Hurting
Facing ugly things

She's raw
Unfiltered
Honest
Letting herself be angry

Realize
You are no man's peace
You *don't* need to be

So keep your intensity
Refuse to play the game
Light an even bigger fire

Under your divine, sacred rage

Your homework is to stay angry
Because if you don't
Who will?

# Mahina

Diving beneath the waning crescent
I'm pulled back to the sand
Once she feels I'm ready

Offering the blood of my womb
To the dark moon who holds me
In her tides, singing

The wind song of the waning gibbous
Who cleanses each crevice
Of this body in sacred salt

Her fullness, returning me
To the truest form of her
The most natural form
Of me

# Not Knowing

how the fog drips to the bottom of the mountain
cascading into a sheet that rests at the water's base
to sit with it
in the not knowing
but feeling
a gray, blurry sky
with streaks of black
nestling from the haze
rolling in
not knowing which moment
but feeling
*soon*

# Not a Martyr

Some things have to be gutted
In order for others to truly grow
When you put fertilizer on plastic grass
You can't expect anything to bloom

If you thought I would stay silent, I can be angry too
If you expected me to play nice, I can be violent too
If you guessed I was a maiden, there's a secret
I've been dying to share

A fox with an oily voice
Serves tea diluted with vinegar
Instead of milk

A maimed eagle circles the forest
Quiet within a tree's perch

Watching the poison brew

*Enough is enough*

Feet extended, wings stretched
She dives
Giving the fox no time to react
To the fanned-out talons suddenly viced around its neck
Much less
The pointed beak sinking into its skull

Void of mercy
She dines, *slowly*
Leaving nothing behind
No fur, no meat, no bones, *no memory*

# La Víctima de Nadie: Una Fantasia?

## *Nobody's Victim: A Fantasy?*

*I am no rapist's victim*
*I am his nightmare*

I went back to the clinic
Made friends with his receptionist

I wasn't the first
Neither was she

We got close
Became sisters

Over time, we found others
Some new survivors, some old

*The bond you never want to share*

His time was coming

He walked out the door that day
But never made it home
When he woke up
He was duct taped to the same table
Where he raped

Her
Me
And all the others

With rocuronium running through his veins
I smiled and pointed to the IV drip
He couldn't move
Was about to feel it all

I was getting hungry
I covered his face with a plastic shopping bag
Tied it around his neck
So he'd be entertained while
My friend and I split a tamale

Once she got bored,
She tore a hole
On the spot of the bag near his mouth
She let him breathe for a moment
Then she grabbed a smaller, smellier bag
*A gift from her dog on their morning walk*

Of course he wouldn't eat it at first
So she took a pair of pliers to his fingernails
The pathetic piece of shit
Complied halfway through the first denailing
She shoved dog shit into his mouth
Laughed as he swallowed
She peeled off the rest of his fingernails and toenails

One
By
One
While I danced to the sound of his screams

It was my turn

I pulled the bag off his head
*But not before choking him a little with it*
He watched as I methodically filed my fingernails
Into sharp points
I wrapped one hand around his throat
Sunk my nails into his grimy skin,
Scooping chunks of his skin and blood,
Which I kept in a jar as a souvenir

With the other hand,
I held a mirror to his face and whispered,
"Me aseguraré de que veas todo"
                        *I'll make sure you see everything*

I grabbed the scalpel from his drawer
She held the mirror inches away from his face
I traced his eyelids with the blade
Making sure he'd never be lucky enough to blink
Ever
Again

You have to understand
I don't want him to die
I want him to live and suffer

I want him to be scarred with constant reminders
Of the way he hurt women
I want every person he meets
To face the disgusting truth
Of a man who will return to the world
As a port-a-potty in his next life

She rummaged through our Mary Poppins bag of
Torture tools
And pulled out a four-inch PVC pipe
She held it like a baseball bat and whacked his shins
*For fun*
We undressed him, flipped him over

I wonder how it feels in comparison
To what we felt

He started to faint from the pain
So I jabbed an EpiPen into his thigh
Whispered, "Ni te atrevas coño"

*Don't you fucking dare*

We took a dinner break
*Arroz con pollo y lentejas*
(Rice with chicken and lentils)
A meal that still makes me salivate

I figured he was hungry too
For something besides dog shit, probably
I pulled out a cleaver from the Mary Poppins bag
While she flipped him on his back
And carefully placed his dick on a cutting board

I might've gotten nauseous
At the familiar sight
*If I hadn't been so damn excited*

With my mother's cleaver
I chopped it into medallion-shaped slices
I picked up each piece with a fork
Served him dinner
Making sure
He'd never hurt another girl again

*She put a tourniquet around it so he wouldn't bleed out*
*We're not psychopaths, ok?*

In a fit of rage,
I bent his fingers and toes backwards
Until the bones broke
I struck his ribs with the PVC pipe
And thought of every girl, every woman
Who has been tortured at the hands
*Of men like him*

We were getting tired
This was getting messy
Before we closed up shop,
We each grabbed a scalpel
Took turns carving into his chest

*HE RAPED ME*
*AND ME*
*AND ME*

*AND ME*
*AND ME*
*AND ME . . .*

Did I mention we taped the whole thing?
It played on a loop
In his waiting room TV
Now everyone will know
His dirty little secret

We're not monsters, you know
We threw him on the porch of the nearest ER
We have *some* decency

No, I don't want him dead
I want him to live on the brink of death
I want him crippled
Unable to fend for himself
He will spend the rest of his life in agony
In as much pain as he can possibly be in *without* dying
Until his pathetic-ness can't take it anymore
He will think about each of us
The same way we've thought of him
All these years

**No soy su víctima**

*I am not your victim*

**Soy su pesadilla**

*I am your nightmare*

# Coming Home

The next Goddess story I tell
Will be about *myself*

How I stopped being ashamed to say *pussy*
Using it to heal myself and every
Woman in the process

I'll tell the story of how my chest was pounding so fast
When I walked in circles through a lightless void
*Searching and searching*
Tearing through people, weed, and material bullshit
Only to ask the same question over and over again
*Am I moving forward? Am I moving at all?*

I got tired
*So tired*
Of fighting
Trudging through muck
Sinking into a hole that just got harder and harder to climb out of
Allowing everyone, *including myself*
To walk all over me

I explored myself
The magic between my legs
When the little twinkles of light
Started to glimmer between my fingertips
Danced along every crevice of my body
I realized
The Goddess that was missing
*Looked a lot like me*

# Wasting Time

*Dedicated to my late grandfather,
Rick Harbottle*

I sit on the edge of the dock
Letting my feet dangle over the water
Watching the sun dance across the tide

I realize that I can't tell
Where my breath ends and the wind begins

I think of you
Somehow you always find me
Whatever lake in the world I visit
No matter how alone I think I am
You're still sitting next to me

I hear the wind whistle
It sounds like Otis Redding
How he could describe
The way you became the lake that day
Far better than I ever will

Tempted to sit until the evening comes
Tempted to make this dock my home

There's a fisherman behind me
Ready to set up his poles
I'm gonna make him wait
I'm not ready to leave you yet

And I'm not okay
But I think I will be

# Grounding

If you stand under a tree
When it's cold and rainy like today
Watch each droplet of water
Roll in slow motion
Off a leaf
And onto your skin

Goosebumps surge across your limbs
When the coolness of the wind
Kisses every hair follicle

Ditch your shoes
To acquaint your feet
With the mud squelching between your toes

Look up
Look down
Graze the rough, scarred bark
And realize
She is healing
Right alongside you

# Heart & Hunter

I remember the day I met her
The woman whose dry, cracked lips held a secret

I remember it looked like it hurt
How the bruises on her hips took shape of the fingers
She so desperately wanted to run from

I remember the night I tried to figure her out
How she'd finish by sobbing into her shirt
Not knowing how much more she could take
Wondering how she was going to make it to tomorrow
Was more frightening than the face she would've given
anything to forget

*Daughter of the moon,*
*I feel her words on my fingertips*
*Ears are listening*
*Tongue – ready to speak*

*Sister of the stars, bring a breath of refreshment*
*With your cool, autumn wind*
*Blowing leaves through her hair*

*Mother of the planets, it's time for something different*

*I'm just an old woman*
*Who's seen too much*
*To put down a pen*

# Maybe If My Mother

*Savasana*: to be in your body

When I stop thinking
Stop racking my brain for the perfect way
To articulate something
Stop searching for words altogether . . . the irony

It looks like swaying my hips in a sensual dance
Instead of stagnant squats and bicep curls – how boring

It looks like eating a chocolate-chip cookie
Instead of scarfing it down in seconds
I take the time to let it melt in my mouth

It looks like an unintentional 30-minute *savasana*
Where I didn't fall asleep
It was just a really good *savasana*

It looks like staring up at the clouds
Finding shapes while I squeeze sand between my toes
When was the last time I did that?

Does your brain ever get in your way?
Mine does

I wax and wane
Just like the moon
Why do I fight it?

Maybe if my mother had been taught
To love herself **first**
I would've welcomed the divinity
Of the blood between my thighs
*Sooner*

# Crawling into a Vagina

Blood drips between her thighs
      His lips purse in disgust

If that liquid is clear and slippery
      He drools in delight

She feeds her baby in public
      He scoffs at the sight, repulsed

Behind closed doors
      He sucks her bare breast *as if starving*

She's a toy to fuck
      Nothing more

But he'll spend his life crawling
      Into a vagina

The same place from which he entered this world

# Done

The fire inside
She spent years
Dumping truckloads of sand onto

To be sweet
To be calm
To be pretty

*No*

She's angry
Wearing the rage of her mother proudly

We've been assaulted, diminished, silenced
Generation after generation

The snake attacks only when provoked
Salivating at the mere thought
Excited to bite
Teeth sink into flesh
Coagulated blood
She wears the venom of her grandmothers proudly

Power
That is not yet mine
Falls into paralysis

Because Goddess is angry
And her children are coming

# Everything's Bigger

How deep is the river
When I'm buried with the bluebonnets
Under hot, Southern clay

Where sky meets gravel
Cowboy country was mine
Because it didn't remind me of anything

Between earth and water
Smoke and sun
Until it feels me
Until it heals me

# We Are Witches

We are Goddesses
We are Warriors
We are Queens

No longer will you silence us
Nor deafen us
Nor blind us

The snake slithering into your bed
Hisses our truth
Our Mother's truth, our Grandmothers' truths

Hand between your teeth
We yank the tongue from your mouth
**Our** turn to speak

Lest you forget
The womb
Your existence comes from

We are Witches
And from ashes
*Through our wombs, we have risen with the moon*

# A Teacher for Life

You've said a few things to me that I'll never forget

Like the time I gestured to my third eye
And you said
*No! Close it! Suck on a lemon!*

Or the time I felt no one was angry except me
And you threw your arms in the air yelling
*Well somebody fucking has to be!*

The 207th time you reminded me
I am Bagalamukhi by saying
*You have to realize you are not sweet!*

My personal favorite
*I don't care how FUCKING flexible you are!*
Because it's funnier without context

Even Saraswati puts on her Kali hat from time to time

30 years from now
I'll remember the way you clicked your tongue
Pausing to *sit with it*
When you said something incredibly profound

40 years from now
I'll remember that your hugs

Smelled like a thousand sticks
Of burned sandalwood incense

50 years from now
I'll still be brewing the perfect cup of chai tea
The one you taught me to make
Back in my 20s

60 years from now
I'll look at my students and their students
And smile at the work our lineage did

Resurrecting the Goddess

# Toes

I used to hate my toes
I thought they were too long
Too bony
Like a monkey

Now I love them
Because they're my mom's toes

It's nice knowing
That a piece of her lives within me

I like looking down
Knowing
She's always there

Holding me up

# Nothing

I want to come from a mental place
Where I have everything
Need nothing

*I have everything, so I need nothing*

I don't need another tattoo
Or another crystal
Or another pair of yoga pants
Or another plant

I'm not going to fill this hole with products
I'm tired of the – *I just need this one thing, then
everything will be perfect*
I am already complete

So if I never get a book deal
If I never go on tour
I'm still whole

I am the universe
She resides within me

If I die tomorrow
I truly feel complete

Even though I didn't travel the world
Even though thousands of women didn't hear my words
I touched who I was meant to touch
I went exactly where I was supposed to go

*I had everything, so I needed nothing*

# If I Could Find the Time

You've heard it before
The definition of insanity
Is doing the same thing, over and over again
Expecting different results
Like waiting
Year after year
Knowing the promises become empty
But secretly hoping you'll surprise me anyway

I always know how it'll play out
Maybe this, hopefully that
*I'll get back to you in a few days*
Every time, I'm disappointed and frustrated
Not even at you, but at *me*

I knew exactly what would happen
I let myself get excited anyway
Maybe it's my fault for always hoping
You'll become someone who you're just . . . not
A mirage of the person I wish you to be

I wonder if you'll regret it someday
If you'll look back on your life
Think you worked too much
Felt like you had to
Thought there was no other choice

I wish I could blame you
But I'm the *daughter of a son of a sailor*

I know you're busy
I know there's always something going on
I know your work is important to you
I understand that
I even respect it

But after all this time
Is it too much to ask
Is it so selfish of me
To want to come first?

There's a pot of coffee in the kitchen
That no one else will drink
It's yours if you want it

I just want you to visit

# Hand to Mouth

and so what if there's tar
in my lungs
as long as there's lemongrass tea
in my throat

# I Think I Could Understand

> I wish they would've taught me how to love myself
> Instead of being ashamed for what I feel

I sensed I disgusted them
For being different, confused
The dramatic burden who *just loved to cry*

I've been angry and harsh, blaming them
Wondering why I never felt listened to

How would I do it differently?
By not having my own

> And no, I won't feel guilty for any of it

But I think I could understand
Support looked different back then
*Keep it hidden – don't let anyone see you break*

So I have to forgive them
And myself, too
Because if I don't
The pattern lives

I don't know if I'll ever feel heard
I think they did the best they could
With the demons they had

And I wish they had been taught to love themselves
Instead of being ashamed for who they are
I wish someone would've held them

The way I want them to hold me

# A Piece of You

I still think about you
Sometimes you visit me in my dreams

I wonder how you're doing
Yet, it feels inappropriate to ask

I hope you're ok
I hope you're happy
I hope you love *every time* like it's the first time

I'll never forget what you gave me
The unconditional comfort
An escape from the blaring sirens that made my ears bleed

Did you know it was what I needed?
Because I never told you
*Instinct* – when you feel it in your bones
But your brain hasn't gotten there yet

Even though we didn't wind up being each other's
There's still a section of my heart
That will always be dedicated

To you

# Because It Does

If you want to care for someone
How they truly need it
Pay attention
To the way they love you

When "how was your day" feels as obligatory
Mundane as taking off your pajamas in the morning
Ask what my least favorite sound was today

Push me – to think, feel, create . . . as if it actually matters

# Golden-Brown Butter

His skin was the color of golden-brown butter
When I put my face on his chest
And his wiry hairs tickled my nose
Every thought I had seemed to melt away

My alarm clock was him
Coiling his body around mine
Pressing his lips against my neck
Brushing shapes along my belly
With the faintest pressure of his fingertips
I almost didn't know his hand was there at all

My mom says, "Todo lo que ella quiere, él lo hace"
("Everything she wants, he does")

He still sings to me every day
Still pets me to sleep every night
He kisses the earth after my feet touch it
And reminds me that his higher power…*is me*

I'll spend the rest of my days swimming in
golden-brown butter

# Shuffling Cards

the Tower
the unmade bed
the me in me, taking advantage
of *whatever* seems too good to be true
one final journey
into the deepest parts of myself
of loving, of living
of reveling in dust

# Cracking Open

*My love is like sitting in a hammock on a soft, spring morning. Neither hot nor cold, but cool enough to wear a cardigan and cover with a blanket. Cozy in the slowness. The edges of the hammock remind you that you are held. My love is like closing eyes when in a gust of wind, stopping to be in the stillness, and only opening the eyes to watch how the wind makes the leaves of the trees dance in her honor. My love is like tasting the cold cup of long forgotten chai tea, still delicious without heat, but you wonder why the last sip can never be as warm as the first. My love is like swatting mosquitoes away because **there's always something,** like not noticing the handful that got to taste you until tomorrow's itchiness pays its visit, overstays its welcome, and reminds you of the hammock's hug and wind's kiss. My love is like wrestling with my dog until we both mutually decide it's time for slobbery licks and butt scratches. It's the hand cramp from journaling all morning. It's the beauty in simplicity, and the knowing that it's anything but...*

# The Baptism

Not upset to stay
Not exactly happy either

**A vagabond knows better than to be attached
to any place**

Walking along the shoreline to clear her head
No phone, no dogs, no swimsuit

The urge to dive into the wet saltiness
Was followed by a *no, you can't, you're in regular clothes*
Which was then followed by a *no, I can do whatever the
hell I want*

**And it came to pass
That she was baptized
In the name of Herself**

Before walking home in her dripping regular clothes
She climbed to the edge of the jetties
To sit with Namaka
Because it wasn't time to leave

*No, not yet*

# When the Moon Rises

*When the moon rises*
*I'll be out of ink*
*Nothing more to say*
*No words left to write*
*Because we'll be together*
*Sisters*
*Hand in hand*

# Note from the Author

As someone who struggles with anxiety and depression, what I notice myself experiencing the most along my mental health journey are extreme highs and lows. If you found any level of enjoyment while reading *When the Moon Rises*, I assume you can relate.

On the good days, I'm in love with my little life. My little candles, yoga blocks, herb garden. I'm grateful for a little extra time because without it, I wouldn't be learning all these painfully pretty things about myself. The fire in the sky heats my little cheeks – *incredible*. Clouds roll in and turn my little world gray – *even better*. Because I'm confident, secure in believing that I'm exactly where I'm supposed to be. Every little thing I'm destined for is on its way, so I write the moon little love letters and she sings me little lullabies.

But on the bad days, I struggle to remind myself that honey and vinegar create balance. The mountain of clothes in the corner of my room doesn't get touched for the 19th day in a row. The number of coins in my piggy bank translates to *I'm a failure*. I can't think of anything besides the fact that I haven't fed myself, but I still don't have the ambition to make it a*ll* the way to the kitchen. My plants deteriorate as a mirror of myself. I can't even forgive myself for not being able to forgive anyone else. On the bad days,

I can't dump out of my head *I make everyone's lives harder simply by being here.*

So I exercise, meditate, go to therapy, journal, nourish *and* treat myself . . . but I don't sleep enough. I tiredly wake, each bad day feeling longer than the last, each moment growing harder to find those little rays of light.

It's on the bad days when I can't seem to remind myself that I'm gonna wanna treasure *this* bad day, because, *someday*, it'll all be worth it.

That's why I wrote this book. To survive. To make it through just one more *little* day. It's so easy to forget that the little things are actually the big things. My little pen, my little notebook, my little heart touching yours. It's medicine.

www.ingramcontent.com/pod-product-compliance
Lightning Source LLC
Chambersburg PA
CBHW072200070526
44585CB00015B/1224